P9-ELR-455

MAJOR LEAGUE DAD

A Daughter's Cherished Memories

Julia Ruth Stevens
with Bill Gilbert

TRIUMPH
BOOKS
CHICAGO

Copyright © 2001 by Julia Ruth Stevens and Bill Gilbert

No part of this publication may be reproduced, stored in a retrieval system, or transmitted, in any form by any means, electronic, mechanical, photocopying, or otherwise, without the prior written permission of the publisher.

Library of Congress Cataloging-in-Publication Data
Stevens, Julia Ruth.
    Major league dad : a daughter's cherished memories / Julia Ruth Stevens with Bill Gilbert
        p. cm.
    ISBN 1-892049-27-9
    l. Ruth, Babe, 1895–1948. 2. Basball players—United States—Biography. 3. Stevens, Julia Ruth. I. Gilbert, Bill, 1931– II. Title

GV865.R8 S75 2001
796.357'092—dc21
[B]   2001016404

This book is available in quantity at special discounts for your group or organization. For further information, contact:
Triumph Books
601 South LaSalle Street
Suite 500
Chicago, Illinois 60605
(312) 939-3330
Fax (312) 663-3557

Printed in the United States of America

ISBN 1-892049-27-9

Interior design by Eileen Wagner

CONTENTS

PHOTO INDEX

PHOTO INDEX

PHOTO INDEX

INTRODUCTION

Julia Ruth Stevens is the daughter of the immortal Babe Ruth, considered by many to be the greatest player in the history of baseball. He is certainly one of the most celebrated personalities in American history.

This is not a baseball book. Instead, with the help of Bill Gilbert, the best-selling author of nineteen books, Julia Ruth Stevens has recorded her fond memories of her father, what life was like with such a famous person, his love for her, and her love for him, which continues to this day.

A New Father

When Mother married Daddy, it was the second marriage for both of them. They each had a daughter from a previous marriage. Daddy adopted me and Mother adopted his daughter, Dorothy. Fortunately for me, no daughter ever had a more caring, loving, natural father than my adoptive father was to me. Unfortunately, Dorothy never achieved that kind of relationship with my mother.

Daddy and his first wife, Helen, separated, and several years later Helen died in a house fire in Boston.

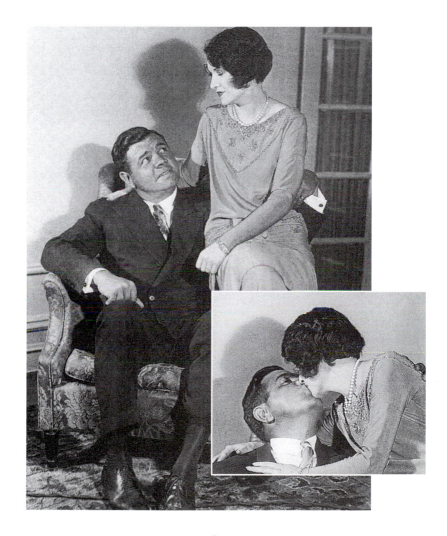

The relationship between Dorothy and Mother was as rocky as my relationship with Daddy was smooth.

I started going to Yankees' games when I was ten or eleven. I knew that Daddy was someone special. But I didn't think of him that way when we were at home. There he was Daddy—a beautiful dancer who loved the fox-trot and delighted in teaching it to me, someone I loved to talk to, to listen to the radio with, someone who cared about me and about Mother and Dorothy. Everywhere we went the crowd worshiped him because he was Babe Ruth. I worshiped him too, but because he was Daddy.

Even though I was not his natural daughter, something happened when I was a teenager that made me feel like I was. I came down with a bad case of strep throat and needed a blood transfusion. We found out that Daddy and I had the same blood type, so he quickly volunteered to donate some of his blood to me. I received the transfusion and made a normal recovery, thanks to him. From that time on, I felt that we were blood relatives, father and daughter, because I had some of his blood in me.

Daddy did something else for me during another childhood illness, something I've always remembered and cherished. I was scheduled to have my tonsils removed, and like any boy or girl of fifteen, I was nervous about it. Just before I was to be wheeled into surgery, Daddy took my hand and held it—right into the operating room. He held hands with me until they put me under with the anesthesia.

That gave me so much confidence at a time when I was frightened. When you're that age and you've never been in a hospital before, much less in an operating room with all of its intimidating equipment and people dressed in surgical clothing and wearing masks, it's a scary time for you. But Daddy was a big help to me in getting through that experience, just by that simple, loving act of holding my hand right up to the minute the surgery began.

Nobody else could have gotten away with it, and nobody else would have been thoughtful enough to even try. But that was Daddy, and that's why I loved him so.

THE BEST FATHER A GIRL COULD ASK FOR

Daddy has been gone for over fifty years now, but I still miss him terribly. I'm sure that those who knew him still miss him, too. Babe Ruth had that effect on you. He was so much more than just one of the greatest athletes of all time. He was also one of the greatest human beings, one of the most dominant personalities in the world, and the best father a girl could ask for. That's how I remember Daddy.

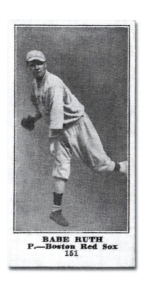

BABE RUTH
P.—Boston Red Sox
151

We had a wonderful relationship. He married my mother, Claire, in 1929, when I was twelve years old. They were married on Opening Day of the 1929 baseball season at Saint Gregory's Church on West 90th Street in New York City. To avoid attracting a large crowd, the ceremony took place at 5:45 A.M. It may have been a good idea, but it didn't work. Hundreds of fans showed up outside the church anyway.

The game was rained out but was played the next day, on Mother's first trip to Yankee Stadium as Mrs. Babe Ruth. Daddy hit the first pitch he saw that day for a home run. As he trotted past third base, he tipped his cap to Mother and blew her a kiss.

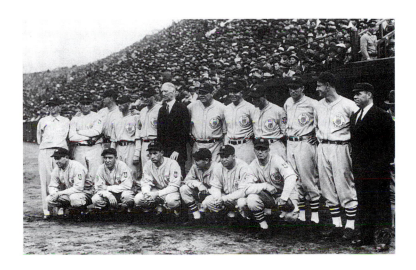

Daddy took me on many of his trips, visiting places any child my age would have given anything to see, including our annual retreat—spring training in Florida. After I graduated from high school in 1934, he brought Mother and me with him when his major league all-star team made a trip to Japan. But that wasn't all. Japan was just one part of that trip. He made it an around-the-world voyage as a graduation present to me.

Daddy gave me a choice—college or that trip. The emphasis on women entering the work force was still a decade away in those years before World War II, so I gladly chose the trip.

It was any seventeen-year-old girl's dream. Besides Japan, we visited France, England, India, and several other countries. I told myself the whole experience was much more of an education than I would have received in a college classroom. I got to see the world the way it used to be and never will be again—World War II changed so many things, even the names of some of the countries we visited.

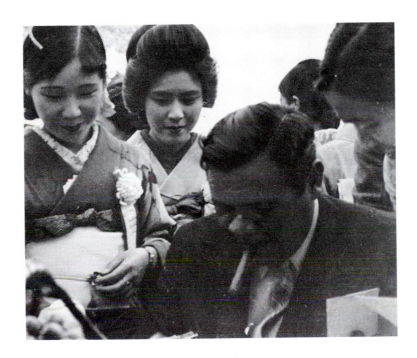

The scenery was so breathtaking, and with not as many automobiles in those years, the pace was slower and the cultures were all distinctive. Now they've all become so westernized that cities in Europe and Asia and South America look the same in so many cases. But not in 1934.

Daddy made my graduation something to remember even before that trip. The Yankees were playing the Browns in St. Louis that day. Daddy had always promised me, "I'll be there for your graduation." And I knew he would be, because Daddy never made a promise he couldn't keep.

Daddy decided to fly back after the game, but the teams didn't want their players flying in those days. Airplanes were still considered too risky. But Daddy took a plane from St. Louis back to Newark, where people landed in those years before LaGuardia and Kennedy airports were built. Dorothy and I went to the airport to meet him.

The plane was late, however, and I finally had to say to Dorothy, "I'm not going to graduate unless I get back to school." I made it back to school—Tisne, a small, private, French school—in time for the start of the ceremony, and took my seat with my classmates in the front row. I looked around anxiously every few minutes, but Daddy still hadn't arrived.

Then I heard a murmur start through the audience, and I turned around and saw Daddy and Mother coming through the door. Daddy was carrying a big bouquet of flowers for me. My name had not been called yet, so he made it there in time to see me receive my diploma.

We didn't know it at the time, but that graduation turned out to be one for the history books. Too many parents could no longer afford to send their children to private schools in the depths of the Great Depression, so the school had to close its doors. We were the school's last graduating class.

A different trip with Daddy produced yet another memorable experience. I used to travel with him on some of the Yankees' road trips. Once when we were in Cleveland for a series with the Indians, Daddy was leading off at first base when Lou Gehrig hit a vicious line drive that hit Daddy in the leg and injured him.

The team was going to Chicago to play the White Sox next, and I was supposed to go there with him too. It was my birthday—July 17—and I was hoping to meet a girlfriend there and enjoy the Chicago World's Fair with her, but Daddy couldn't make the trip. He was confined to his hotel room with his leg propped up and covered with ice packs to reduce the swelling.

He gave me a beautiful diamond pin for my birthday and then said, "Now, I want you to go on to Chicago and meet your girlfriend and have a good time at the World's Fair. I'll see you in a few days." So that's what I did.

That was so typical of Daddy. He was always thinking of me, and of others, too.

BABE RUTH
ON THE FIELD

I was always so thrilled when Daddy would hit a home run and sixty thousand fans would stand up, cheering and yelling his name—*my father's name*—in Yankee Stadium. Only a few people ever experience that thrill. I don't have words to describe it. I was so proud of him.

If he struck out and they booed him, it didn't hurt me. It just made me mad. I wanted to slug every one of them. My feeling was, "How dare you?"

Despite all his home runs and his greatness as a hitter and an outfielder, Daddy was proudest of his pitching. He never failed to talk about his pitching records. If somebody else didn't mention them, he would. And no wonder. Beginning with his first full season for the Boston Red Sox in 1915, he won 94 games, even though he was a full-time pitcher for only three full seasons. For the rest of his time with the Red Sox, until he joined the Yankees in 1920, he divided his time between the outfield and first base.

He was so proud of his World Series pitching. For forty-four years he held the Series record for the longest string of shutout innings. And he beat the man many consider the greatest pitcher in history, Walter Johnson, six times in nine games.

How do I know all this? Because Daddy told me.

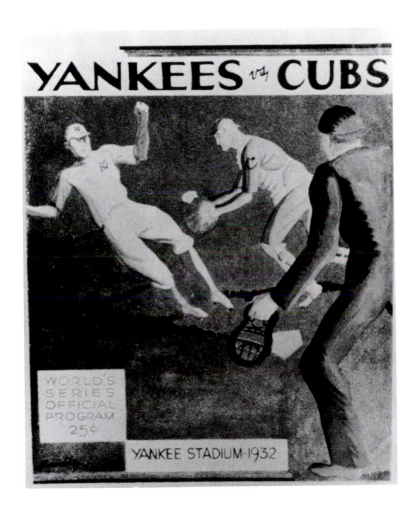

FATHER KNOWS BEST

Daddy insisted that Dorothy and I finish high school and perform well there. One reason for this, I'm sure, is that Daddy deeply regretted his own lack of education. His parents sent him to a reform school, Saint Mary's Industrial School for Boys, when he was only seven years old. They called him "incorrigible." He stayed there until he was nineteen. When he left, it was to become a professional baseball player, thanks to one of the men at Saint Mary's, Brother Matthias.

In all of his years at Saint Mary's, his parents almost never brought him home—except when they needed him to help with some of the work around the bar his father owned, near the site of the present-day Orioles ballpark, Camden Yards. Daddy was born on the very grounds where the Orioles now play, and lived there until he was "put away" at age seven. His parents never once came to bring him home for Christmas, even though they lived in Baltimore, the same city where Saint Mary's was located.

47

Brother Matthias and his colleagues did the best they could at Saint Mary's, but in the early 1900s no boy was going to get a high-quality education at what was, after all, a "reform school"—not like what he could receive in a normal high school, public or private.

That's why Daddy made certain that Dorothy and I finished high school, which not every boy or girl got to do at that time. These were the Depression years. A lot of kids had to drop out of school to help support their parents. But we were financially comfortable thanks to Daddy's great success in baseball, so Dorothy and I were able to finish high school. Daddy wouldn't have had it any other way.

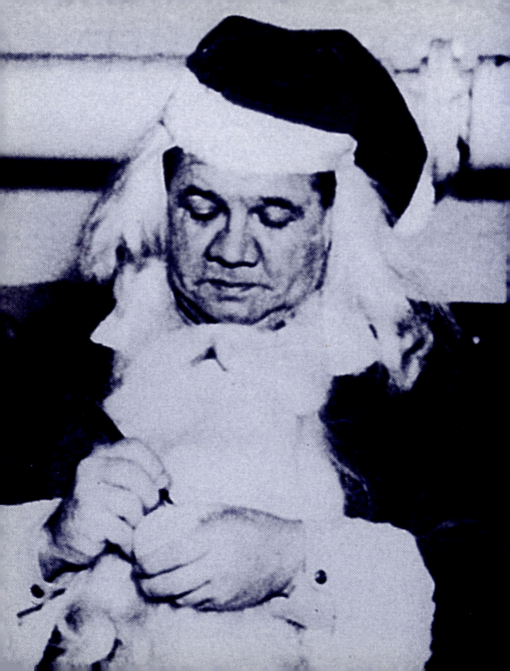

CHRISTMAS

Every Christmas with Daddy was memorable. This was probably another result of his bleak family life as a child. I think Daddy loved Christmas more than any other time of the year because, as a husband and father, he had a family, something he never had when he was growing up. There was my mother, my sister, and me, Mother's two brothers, and my grandmother—seven of us including Daddy—all living in our beautiful, fourteen-room apartment on Riverside Drive, in a lovely setting along the Hudson River.

I'm sure Daddy's enthusiasm about the holidays stemmed from all those Christmases when he was left abandoned by his parents at Saint Mary's. When he finally became a member of a family—a *real* family—and got to exchange gifts and trim the tree and carve the turkey, it's a safe bet that he was experiencing those things for the first time.

He loved everything about Christmas, starting with trimming the tree. He did it all himself. He didn't want any help. He was meticulous about it. The icicles had to be put on one strand at a time. After the tree was completely decorated, we'd turn on the Christmas tree lights, turn out all the other lights, and sit in the darkened room, admiring the tree.

And Daddy's face would beam with his boyish enthusiasm.

A FAMILY FEUD WITH THE GEHRIGS

Daddy loved Lou Gehrig, and so did all of us. And Lou and his wife, Ellie, felt the same way about our family too. But a silly little incident involving my sister Dorothy caused a breach between Daddy and Lou and the two families that lasted for seven unfortunate years. It was the same kind of misunderstanding that often happens in families, in neighborhoods, and among friends.

Dorothy and I, especially Dorothy, loved to visit the Gehrigs up in New Rochelle because Lou's mother cooked such delicious German meals and rich desserts. Dorothy was invited to spend the weekend with the Gehrigs, and she took play clothes instead of good ones. Before she left, I asked her, "Are you going to take *those* clothes?"

She said, "Yes. We're just going to be playing."

Lou's mother mistakenly thought that Dorothy's play clothes, some of which were even torn, were what Mother normally dressed her in. Later she said something to the wife of one of the other Yankee players about "poor little underfed, badly dressed Dorothy." Of course that player's wife told another player's wife, and the gossip spread at the speed of, well, at the speed of gossip.

When the story reached Mother, she became furious. In later years she told me, "I did just what any other outraged wife would do. I told Daddy that Dorothy was never going to New Rochelle again in her life." And she didn't, not as long as Mother had anything to say about it.

That's not the way Dorothy tells the story in a very negative, bitter book she wrote. But that's what Mother told me, and I believe Mother. She said Daddy told Lou about it, and said, "Never speak to me again off the ball field."

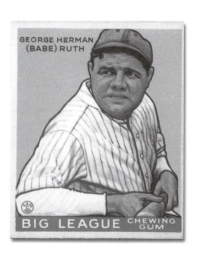

Gehrig   France Laux - Babe R...
            Sports Announcer
            June 7th 1930
                                Bob Arte...

They didn't speak except on the field for seven years, including the last several years of Daddy's playing career—not until after Lou took himself out of the lineup in 1939. A famous moment in baseball history brought them back together.

It was July 4, 1939. The Yankees were playing the Washington Senators in a holiday doubleheader, something that baseball fans all over America used to be able to look forward to on Memorial Day, the Fourth of July, and Labor Day.

More than sixty thousand fans showed up at Yankee Stadium, including Mother, Dorothy, and me, but not for the Independence Day celebration. It was "Lou Gehrig Day." By now the world knew that Lou had a terminal disease, amyotrophic lateral sclerosis, known forever since as "Lou Gehrig's disease."

Many of Lou's teammates from over the years were there, including Bob Meusel, Tony Lazzeri, Joe Dugan, and Waite Hoyt. Lou was in uniform, the familiar Yankee pin-stripes with his No. 4 on the back. Mel Allen was the master of ceremonies for this tribute to Lou.

We knew Daddy was down there somewhere, but he wasn't visible on the field. He must have been in the dugout or the dressing room. We could hear the fans around us asking each other where "the Babe" was.

Then we saw some motion around home plate, amid the hush that echoed throughout Yankee Stadium, "The House That Ruth Built." We saw Daddy walking out of the dugout and toward the plate in a light summer sports jacket and a white sports shirt left open at the neck.

He went straight to Lou, who was standing near the plate, and squeezed him in a giant bear hug, the kind that only Daddy could give. And Lou hugged him back.

The feud was over, and these two men who had once been so close were suddenly, in a flash, close friends once again.

DANCING WITH DADDY

Of all the dances that were popular in the 1920s and '30s, Daddy loved the fox-trot most of all. I delighted in gliding around our living room with him while a record— one of the old, big, round ones—played on our phonograph machine. I had very few dates that I enjoyed dancing with as much as I did with Daddy. He had a superb sense of timing on the dance floor, maybe the same timing that made him such a great pitcher and hitter. I just loved to dance with him.

It was a good thing he was such a good dancer. He felt a great enthusiasm for music, but he couldn't carry a tune in a basket! So the dancing filled that void for him.

It was such a lot of fun just to be with him. We went to
football games together, and hockey games and bowling—
but not to the movies. Daddy avoided the movies, as well
as reading. He was afraid those activities might harm his
eyes and thus interfere with his baseball performance.
Today we know better, but back then we didn't, so Daddy
insisted on protecting his vision. He allowed himself to see
only six or seven movies a year, at a time when many
Americans were seeing a lot more than that because
movies were still a relatively new form of entertainment.

We even had a special time together—just the two of us—on those days when Daddy would go hunting or fishing. He always liked to get an early start, so he'd get up early in the morning and leave at about 5:00 A.M. to get ahead of the traffic.

He'd come into my room and say softly, "Hey, want some breakfast?" We'd go into the kitchen and Daddy would fix breakfast for us. And he had his own specialty— a Babe Ruth original. He'd take a slice of bread and butter it, and then brown it in a frying pan. Then he'd cut a hole in the middle of it and turn it over and drop an egg into it. He'd fry the egg and fry some baloney to go with it. Not bacon—it had to be baloney.

I'm not a breakfast eater and never have been, but those breakfasts that Daddy fixed were delicious. We'd sit down, just the two of us, and talk and eat, what today we would call "quiet time" together.

Then we'd kiss each other goodbye and he'd say, "Well, thanks for the company." And then he'd head off to go fishing or hunting, and I'd head back to bed.

DADDY THE DISCIPLINARIAN

People used to say that Daddy wouldn't have made a good baseball manager. He had trouble controlling himself, so how could he control twenty-five players? But I know the answer to that question: discipline.

He was a disciplinarian as a father; not harsh, but strict enough to make sure Dorothy and I behaved ourselves. He was a strict father, but a good one.

I might not have appreciated it at the time, but when I became a parent myself, I realized I was doing just about the same things he did. I had strict rules for my son, Tom, on what time he should be home and how he should behave, and I got those values and attitudes from Daddy when I was growing up.

Any time I went out on a date in my teens, Daddy would tell me in no uncertain terms, "Now, you have to be home by midnight." And that wasn't a rule only when I was a teenager. It remained a rule until I got married. And my dates always made sure to get me home on time.

How strict was he? He forced me to break an engagement when I was twenty years old. He told me, "No girl has enough sense to get married until she's twenty-five."

He was basing his attitude on experience. He married Helen, his first wife, at twenty, and it didn't work out. Mother was a teenager when she married for the first time, and that didn't work out either. So Daddy was speaking from experience and taking this firm stand because he honestly believed it was best for me as his daughter.

When I did get married, I was twenty-three. Apparently, Daddy figured that was close enough.

A Patriotic American

There is a tragic P.S. to the story of our trip to Japan in 1934, when Daddy took me along and then toured the world with me as my high school graduation present.

It happened seven years later. On the evening of December 7, 1941, just after the awful news came over the radio about the Japanese attack on Pearl Harbor, Daddy went almost berserk at the idea that anything like that could happen. He couldn't believe that the nation that had treated his fellow American all-stars and him like heroes had just attacked our country.

He grabbed some of his souvenirs from that trip and threw them right out the window of the apartment that he and Mother still shared on Riverside Drive—and they lived on the fourteenth floor! He didn't want anything to do with those souvenirs and awards. They landed in Riverside Park below.

Daddy was forty-six years old when World War II started, too old for military service. So he did the next best thing: he served his country by making appearances all over America, promoting the sale of war bonds, and visiting with our GIs.

One of his appearances on the home front was at his baseball "home," Yankee Stadium, on August 23, 1942, when he and Walter Johnson faced each other on the field for the last time. The two players staged a "duel" before a Yankees-Senators game. The purpose of the match-up— between one of the greatest pitchers in history and one of the best hitters of all time—was to raise money for the Army and Navy Relief Fund, which benefited women and children who were widowed and orphaned by the war.

Daddy hit a "home run" into the seats in right field. When a reporter asked Johnson, one of the grandest gentle-men ever to play the game, if he "grooved one" [threw an

easy pitch] so that Daddy could hit it out of the park, Johnson replied, "The fans didn't come here to see me strike out Babe Ruth. They came to see him hit a home run."

Daddy made a surprise appearance in Washington, D.C., during the war at the request of Shirley Povich, the Hall of Fame sports columnist for *The Washington Post.* Povich had organized an exhibition game at Griffith Stadium in Washington between the Senators and a team of navy all-stars including Bob Feller, Phil Rizzuto, and Dom DiMaggio.

Povich, the most modest man you'd ever want to meet, made it a star-spangled event by convincing Kate Smith and Bing Crosby to appear. Smith stood behind second base and sang "God Bless America," and Crosby sang some of his biggest hits.

Then, for Povich's grand finale, Daddy came trotting out of the Senators' dugout on the first-base side, waved to the crowd, and trotted around the bases. The fans, starved for something to cheer about during those dark days in the first year of the war, roared for him.

The event raised $2 million and paid for a navy cruiser. It was the second largest amount of money ever raised through a sports event until that time, topped only by the second Dempsey-Tunney fight.

Daddy was involved in the war in another unique way. During the final year of the war, as the situation grew more desperate for Japan's fighting forces, their soldiers would go into hiding on the various Pacific islands we took. They tried to anger the American soldiers and marines by yelling, "To hell with Babe Ruth!"

They thought that by insulting our national hero they could aggravate the Americans so much that our troops would stick their heads out of their foxholes to respond, and then the Japanese snipers could pick them off, one by one.

There is no evidence that the trick ever worked, but it certainly was a compliment to Daddy.

DADDY'S LOVE FOR KIDS

Kids—his own and everyone else's—were the delight of Daddy's life. He loved them dearly, and they knew it.

In addition to showering Dorothy and me with all the love and attention we could ask for, he did the same with other kids. He even adopted a "mascot," a three-year-old boy who captivated Daddy when he saw him playing baseball with his father in a park along Riverside Drive, near our apartment. His name was Ray Kelly.

Daddy took such a liking to him after seeing him hit and throw with some obvious talent that he invited little Ray and his father to the Yankees game the next day. They couldn't believe this was happening, of course, but it was, and it became the start of a close, ten-year friendship between Daddy and this cute little boy. He became known forevermore as Daddy's "mascot."

Ray got to sit in the Yankees' dugout before games, and Daddy even took him on some road trips. One of

those trips included Daddy's famous "called shot" home run in the 1932 World Series in Chicago. And yes, Ray says Daddy definitely called his shot.

Ray once told a television reporter, "He [Ruth] was more than a hero to me for the ten years I spent with him. He was almost like a father. What more than that can I say? He was a loving father. . . . And as far as I was concerned, he always acted around me like a big kid. He was a jovial individual, loved everybody, and particularly loved children. He never had a bad word to say about anybody in my presence. He was just a wonderful human being."

A Japanese writer once said that Daddy's love of the Japanese children on our trip there in 1934 made a lasting impression on him. Even more than sixty years later, Kazuo Sayama said, "When he came to Japan in 1934, the first thing he did was to spend some time with the children. They were at the pier, you know, the Yokohama Pier. They were lined up in baseball uniforms. And the first thing Babe did was to talk to them, play with them, you know, and carry them in his arms. And not only that, he encouraged other baseball players, American players, to do the same. The first thing he showed was his love for the children, his love for the Japanese, and we all loved *him*."

There was another child who developed a love for Daddy that lasted a lifetime. He was an eleven-year-old boy named Johnny Sylvester. He was seriously ill from either blood poisoning or injuries suffered when he was thrown from a horse, depending on which version of the story you hear or read. His father wrote Daddy a letter asking for his autograph, and Daddy responded with a lot more than that: an autographed baseball, another signed by Rogers Hornsby (the manager of the St. Louis Cardinals who had just defeated our Yankees in the 1926 World Series), and a personal visit.

Daddy got into his car and drove to Essex Falls, New Jersey, and visited Johnny in his home on Roseland Avenue. The boy had not been doing well, but his father later told Daddy that Johnny started getting better immediately after that visit. He called it a miracle.

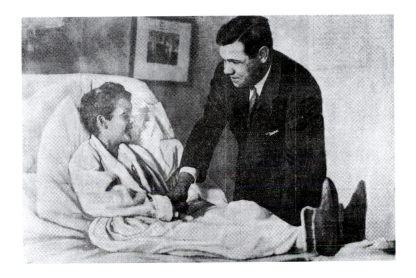

Twenty-two years later, when Johnny was president of a packing machinery company in New York and Daddy was stricken with cancer, Johnny visited him on Riverside Drive. We'll never know if Johnny's visit helped Daddy the way Daddy's visit helped him, but this much we *do* know: after Johnny's visit, Daddy lived for another few months.

DADDY'S DISAPPOINTMENT

Anyone hates to see his or her parent go through a difficult time, and I watched Daddy as he went through the greatest disappointment of his life: when no team in baseball would hire him as a manager.

He never was one to sit around and feel sorry for himself, but he wanted to manage a team more than anything else in the world after his playing days were over. And baseball never gave him a chance.

Following the final blow in 1946, when Larry MacPhail snubbed him for a second time, passing him over for the Yankee job after doing the same thing when he was running the Dodgers, Daddy just sat down in our living room and cried.

Daddy's lifestyle and his fondness for bright lights and associated attractions were well known. His friend, authorized biographer, and occasional nighttime accomplice, columnist Bob Considine, once wrote that Daddy "thought every night was New Year's Eve." That reputation led to the charge that he couldn't have handled a team. According to some people, if he couldn't manage himself, how could he manage a whole team?

That charge is not only unfair, it's also baseless—because he never was given the opportunity to show if he could manage. So how can you tell whether he would have been good at it?

I always thought he deserved the chance, at least as much as some of the other former players who have become managers did. And if he fell flat on his face, that would be it. But I'm convinced he would have been a good manager, and a winning one.

Several New York newspaper men told me in later years that the real reason Daddy never got to manage a team was because his players, knowing he was paid high salaries during his own playing years, would have demanded the same thing for themselves. That sounds far-fetched to me, but in those days, owners were capable of thinking like that.

DADDY'S DISAPPOINTMENT

I think Daddy would have been a good manager, and I have something to base my belief on. I can remember times when he would come home from a game and, if the Yankees had lost, he'd start to analyze it. He rarely brought the game home with him, but from time to time he'd be upset because he thought we could have won if the team had done some things differently. He'd say to us, "Now if this had been done and that would have been done, we would have won that game."

He was so baseball-wise. This is the same man that everyone agreed never threw to the wrong base, was never out of position, was a smart pitcher, and was one of the most intelligent players of his time. And I know from the way he raised Dorothy and me that he had what it takes to be a disciplinarian.

There's one more reason Daddy would have been a good manager, and it's something many of the men who have been managers lacked: he would have been what baseball people call "a player's manager." His players would have appreciated his treatment of them so much that they would have wanted to win for him. And that makes a manager successful. That's why so many managers don't succeed.

He was deeply disappointed that he never got to manage and that baseball seemed to turn its back on him again. His final rejection came less than two years before he passed away. When Daddy died, the official reason given was cancer. But I think he also died of a broken heart.

SEALS STADIUM AUGUST 23, 1947
San Francisco, California

WHEN DADDY DIED

When Daddy Died

On the day Daddy left the hospital after his first surgery for throat cancer in 1946, I was packing his belongings in his room. I happened to look out the window as he was being helped into the car for the ride back to his apartment. I was struck by how frail he looked, this formerly robust man. I started to cry. It was just so sad. It just tore me up.

He remained mercifully unaware of the nature of his illness, and so did Mother. I called her in the early stages of his illness and asked, "What is wrong with Daddy?"

She said, "They don't seem to know."

When he entered the Sloan-Kettering Memorial Hospital for Cancer and Allied Diseases in 1948, not long before he died, he asked those around him, "What are they bringing me in here for?"

Daddy died on August 16, 1948. Jack Lait, the editor of the *New York Daily Mirror* and author of a popular column called "Broadway and Elsewhere," wrote that "Every newspaperman in New York knew for years that Babe Ruth had cancer of the throat. Yet that was never written. We knew he did not suspect, and [we] feared that the dreaded word would break him down."

For that reason, the New York writers and broadcasters voluntarily kept the word about the nature of Daddy's disease out of the papers and off the air. Maybe that couldn't happen today, but it could in the 1940s, and did. It was a noble conspiracy based on the honor and integrity of the reporters and their genuine love for Daddy. I learned about this voluntary silence only in recent years.

The April after Daddy died, the Yankees erected a monument to his memory in center field, next to the ones for Lou Gehrig and Miller Huggins. Mother walked out to center field with the governor, Thomas Dewey, and the mayor of New York City, William O'Dwyer, and all the players on the Yankees and the Washington Senators, that day's opponents. She pulled a cord that lowered the cloth covering the monument. On the facing was a plaque that read:

George Herman "Babe" Ruth. 1895–1948.
A great ballplayer. A great man. A great American.
Erected by the Yankees and the New York Baseball Writers.
April 19, 1949.

As his daughter, I know they could have added three other words: *a great father.*